Unapologetically me : A Guide for Young Ladies to Embrace Their Identity and Style

LILIAN M.

Published by GORDON MILLS, 2024.

While every precaution has been taken in the preparation of this book, the publisher assumes no responsibility for errors or omissions, or for damages resulting from the use of the information contained herein.

UNAPOLOGETICALLY ME : A GUIDE FOR YOUNG LADIES TO EMBRACE THEIR IDENTITY AND STYLE

First edition. November 4, 2024.

Copyright © 2024 LILIAN M..

ISBN: 979-8224707522

Written by LILIAN M..

Table of Contents

	1
Introduction	3
Chapter 1	7
The Journey of Self-Discovery	8
Understanding Your Values	9
Identifying Your Strengths and Passions	11
Creating a Vision for Yourself	13
Chapter 2	15
Building Unbreakable Confidence	16
Silencing Self-Doubt	17
Body Positivity and Acceptance	19
Setting Boundaries and Standing Firm	21
Chapter 3	23
Defining Your Personal Style	24
Finding Your Fashion Personality	25
Fashion Fundamentals: Building a Wardrobe	27
Accessorizing with Purpose	29
Chapter 4	31
Celebrating Cultural Heritage in Style	32
Incorporating Cultural Elements into Your Wardrobe	33
Understanding the Stories Behind Fabrics	35
Making a Statement with Tradition	37
Chapter 5	39
Navigating Trends and Staying True to Yourself	40
Trends vs. Timeless: Choosing What's Right for You	41
Social Media Pressure and Authenticity	43
Curating Your Own Style Inspiration Board	45
Chapter 6	47
Becoming the Best Version of Yourself	48
Daily Habits for Confidence and Self-Care	49
Setting Goals and Staying Motivated	51

Giving Back and Inspiring Others 53
Conclusion.. 55

Unapologetically Me

A Guide for Young Ladies to Embrace Their Identity and Style

LILIAN M.

Introduction

Alright, let's talk about what it really means to be "unapologetically you." I'm not talking about the version of you that bends to make others comfortable or the one that gets drowned out by the noise of other people's expectations. No, I'm talking about the woman who feels like a fire on the inside—who knows there's something unique and precious about her, even if the world isn't always ready for it. That's the version of you that I want to see.

See, I've learned that the world has all sorts of ideas about who we should be. They want us to fit into neat little boxes that feel safe and easy. Maybe they want you to smile a certain way, dress a certain way, stay quiet when you want to roar. They'll say, "Why don't you try being more like this or that?" But you're not a piece of clay waiting to be molded by other people's hands. You're not here to blend in. You're here to break free, to be seen, to stand firm. And that journey—that unapologetic stance—is something that nobody can define for you. It's something you build with every choice, every moment you say, "This is who I am."

When I look back at the different stages of my own life, I can tell you it wasn't easy to hold on to my identity. From growing up in a tight-knit neighborhood where everyone knew my business, to navigating rooms where I often felt like I didn't quite belong—I had to constantly remind myself of who I was. Sometimes, I stumbled. I tried to fit in. I tried to be what other people wanted me to be. But each time, I felt a little piece of myself slip away. I'd look in the mirror and ask, "Who am I doing this for?" And each time, the answer was never quite right until I decided that I was doing it for me.

Here's the truth: Finding and embracing your true self is messy. It's not this polished journey with a perfect ending. No, it's raw, it's vulnerable, and sometimes it's uncomfortable as hell. You'll be second-guessing yourself, you'll make mistakes, you'll stumble. But every step in that journey is worth it because every step gets you closer to that version of yourself who is bold, radiant, and unwavering. That version of you doesn't shrink to fit someone else's story. She writes her own.

Now, if we're going to do this, if we're going to peel back the layers and get real, we've got to start with one basic question: Who are you? No, really—who are you? Strip away the titles, the achievements, the things people say about you. Who's that person beneath it all? You see, if you don't know her yet, then all the clothes, the makeup, the social media posts won't ever feel right. They'll feel like costumes. So let's start there, with the courage to get to know her, to accept her, flaws and all.

And let me tell you, this is not about following trends or meeting expectations. This is about learning how to honor that voice inside that says, "This is what feels right to me." It's about stepping out of the shadows of what other people think and standing tall in what you know. That's not arrogance—that's confidence. And if there's one thing I know, it's that the world desperately needs more women who are confident in who they are.

What's beautiful about being unapologetically you is that you don't need permission. You don't need someone else to validate you, or tell you, "Yes, you're doing it right." Because here's the thing: There is no "right" way to be you. There's only your way. And yes, that's going to mean making choices that other people might not understand. It might mean wearing that outfit that you love but others think is too bold. It might mean pursuing a career path that doesn't make sense to anyone else but fills your heart with purpose. And it definitely means having the courage to look at yourself in the mirror and say, "I am enough," even when the world tries to tell you otherwise.

Growing up, I was no stranger to expectations. Everywhere I went, people had ideas about who I should be, how I should act. But every single one of those expectations was like a little weight, pressing down, chipping away at what I knew to be true about myself. And at some point, you have to decide that enough is enough. You have to decide that the only expectations that matter are your own. Because at the end of the day, you're the one who has to live with the choices you make. You're the one who has to find peace in who you are.

When you choose to embrace yourself, when you let yourself be seen—really seen—there's a shift that happens. It's like the world around you starts to bend to your will. Suddenly, you're not waiting for approval, you're not hiding in the background, you're stepping forward. And you're saying, "This is who I am, take it or leave it." And that kind of authenticity? It's magnetic. People are drawn to it because deep down, everyone wishes they had the courage to do the same.

So let's get real. Being unapologetically you doesn't mean you're perfect. It doesn't mean you have it all figured out. It means you're willing to show up, flaws and all. It means you're willing to do the hard work of facing yourself, of learning to love the parts of you that maybe you've kept hidden. It means looking at the things that scare you about yourself and saying, "I'm not running from this anymore." Because true confidence isn't about pretending you don't have weaknesses. True confidence is knowing you have them and deciding they don't make you any less.

This journey we're about to embark on together? It's not just about style, though that's part of it. It's about finding a style that feels like an extension of your soul, a style that reflects who you are, not who you think you're supposed to be. It's about the power that comes from putting on that outfit and feeling like you're stepping into your own skin, fully, completely. Clothes are just one way we get to express ourselves, and when you're rooted in who you are, style becomes a tool, not a mask.

Every time you dress, every time you make a choice that reflects who you are, you're telling the world a story. And that story should be yours. Not your mother's, not your friends', not society's. Yours. The beauty of being unapologetically you is that you get to own every chapter of that story. The triumphs, the mistakes, the awkward moments, the times you took a risk and fell flat on your face—all of it is part of your journey. And when you embrace that, you realize that nobody can take that away from you.

So here's what I want you to know as we start this journey: You have every right to take up space. You have every right to say, "This is who I am, and I'm proud of it." The world might not always understand it. People might question it. But none of that matters, because you know in your heart that you are living your truth. And that truth? It's worth more than anyone else's approval.

If you're ready, then let's go. Let's go on this journey of peeling back the layers, of getting comfortable with every part of who you are. Let's build a life that isn't dictated by what others think but instead guided by what feels right to you. Because, at the end of the day, there's no one else who can be you, and that is your greatest power.

Chapter 1

The Journey of Self-Discovery

Understanding Your Values

Alright, let's talk about what really drives you. Not the goals that sound good on paper, or the dreams that other people handed to you—no, I mean those core values, the ones that light a fire in your heart and shape every decision you make. See, your values aren't just a list of nice ideas you jot down on a piece of paper. They're the very foundation of who you are. They're the reasons you feel proud of yourself when no one else is looking, the things that push you to stand firm when the world tries to shake you.

To understand your values, you've got to look deep within, past the noise of other people's opinions. Ask yourself, "What's truly important to me?" Not to your friends, not to your family, not to society—to *you.* Maybe it's honesty. Maybe it's compassion. Maybe it's justice. Whatever it is, that's your anchor. That's what keeps you grounded when life tries to knock you off balance. When you know your values, you start to understand why you feel at peace with some decisions and deeply uneasy with others. Your values become your compass, pointing you towards the choices that align with who you are.

Now, here's the tricky part: sometimes, the world will ask you to compromise those values. There will be moments when you're tempted to bend, to twist yourself into someone else's shape to fit in. But every time you do that, you lose a piece of yourself. Holding onto your values, especially when it's difficult, is the ultimate act of self-respect. It's saying to the world, "This is what I stand for, and I won't back down."

And let's be real—understanding your values isn't something you do once and then forget. Life has a way of testing you, pushing you, challenging those very beliefs. And in those moments, you have to dig deep. You have to remember that these values are not just words. They're a part of you. They're what make you **you.**

Identifying Your Strengths and Passions

If we're going to build an authentic life, we need to know what makes you unique. And I'm not just talking about talents you can list on a résumé. I mean those natural gifts, those passions that make you feel alive. The things that, when you're doing them, time just slips away. Those are your strengths. Those are your passions. They are clues, leading you towards the life you're meant to live.

Finding your strengths starts with paying attention to those moments when you feel completely in your element. Maybe it's the way you can bring people together, or the way you light up when you're working on something creative. Whatever it is, embrace it. Don't ignore it. Don't brush it off as unimportant. Those things that come naturally to you—that's where your power lies. That's what makes you different from everyone else, and that difference? That's a gift.

And here's the thing about strengths: they're not always obvious. Sometimes, we've been told for so long that certain things about us aren't "good enough" that we forget how powerful they actually are. Maybe you've been told you're too sensitive, but that sensitivity is what allows you to connect deeply with others. Maybe you've been told you're too bold, but that boldness is what's going to help you stand up for what's right. So, take a moment to reflect on the parts of yourself that you might have been hiding or downplaying. Those could be the very strengths that set you apart.

Now, once you know your strengths, start thinking about what you're passionate about. What makes you feel excited? What could you talk about for hours without getting tired? Those passions are like little signposts, pointing you toward the work, the people, the places that will bring you joy and fulfillment. And remember, just because something doesn't seem "practical" doesn't mean it isn't valuable. Passion is a kind of energy, and that energy can drive you to places you never imagined.

Creating a Vision for Yourself

Now that you're getting a sense of your values and your strengths, it's time to create a vision. Not some vague dream, not a "maybe someday" kind of goal, but a real, tangible vision of the woman you want to become. Imagine her. Picture what she stands for, what she's accomplished, how she moves through the world. That vision isn't just a wish; it's a roadmap. It's a declaration of who you are and where you're going.

Creating a vision starts with asking yourself some big questions. What kind of life do you want to lead? What kind of impact do you want to make? Who are the people you want by your side, the ones who will push you to grow? Your vision should be a reflection of everything you value, everything you're passionate about. It should be something that fills you with excitement and maybe a little bit of fear. Because if it doesn't scare you, you're not dreaming big enough.

Once you have that vision, don't just tuck it away. Write it down. Make it real. Put it somewhere you'll see it every day. Let it remind you why you're putting in the work, why you're making the choices you're making. That vision is your north star. It's what will keep you moving forward when things get tough, when the path isn't clear, when you're not sure if you're on the right track.

And here's the thing—your vision doesn't have to be perfect, and it doesn't have to stay the same. Life will change. You will change. Your dreams might shift. But that's okay, because the core of your vision will always be rooted in who you are. As long as you're true to your values, your strengths, your passions, you'll always be moving in the right direction.

Chapter 2

Building Unbreakable Confidence

Silencing Self-Doubt

Let's get one thing straight right off the bat—self-doubt is a universal experience. I don't care who you are or what you've accomplished; that little voice of doubt finds a way to creep in. Maybe it questions your worth, maybe it's whispering that you're not smart enough, not pretty enough, not "something" enough. And for too long, we've let that voice run the show. But here's the thing: you don't have to listen to it. You can train yourself to recognize that voice, acknowledge it, and then shut it down.

Silencing self-doubt starts with recognizing it as just a thought, not a fact. Think about that for a moment. Just because a thought pops into your head doesn't mean it's the truth. Maybe somewhere along the line, someone made you feel small, or maybe you've picked up a habit of being overly critical of yourself. But that's just programming. You can rewrite that script. Whenever that voice of self-doubt creeps in, take a moment to question it. Ask yourself, "Is this really true? Or is this just fear talking?" Nine times out of ten, you'll find it's the latter.

One of the best ways to silence that voice is to fill your mind with positivity. Surround yourself with people who lift you up, with affirmations that remind you of your strength, and with actions that build your confidence. It's not about pretending to be perfect; it's about giving yourself permission to be proud of who you are, flaws and all. Practice speaking kindly to yourself. I mean, think about it—would you ever speak to a friend the way you sometimes speak to yourself? Of course not. So why not extend that same kindness inward?

And listen, building confidence isn't a switch you flip overnight. It's a practice. Every time you face that self-doubt head-on, every time you push through it, you're teaching yourself that you're stronger than those negative thoughts. Confidence isn't about never feeling insecure. It's about feeling that insecurity, acknowledging it, and choosing to move forward anyway. That's where real strength comes from.

Body Positivity and Acceptance

The truth is, we live in a world that's constantly telling us we're not enough. Not thin enough, not curvy enough, not young enough. It's exhausting, and it's unfair. But here's what I've come to realize: you get to decide how you feel about your body. Not the media, not society, not some ideal that changes with every decade. **You** get to decide.

Body positivity isn't about loving every single thing about yourself every day. It's about respect. It's about recognizing that your body, just as it is right now, is worthy of love and care. Think of all the incredible things your body does for you every single day. It carries you, it supports you, it lets you experience life. That's something worth celebrating. And sure, maybe there are things you'd like to change, and that's okay. But start with appreciation. Start with respect.

Sometimes, body positivity gets misunderstood as "just love yourself." But it's more than that. It's about challenging the standards that make you feel like you have to be anything other than what you are. It's about unlearning all those messages that made you believe you needed to fit into a certain mold to be beautiful. Beauty is diverse, and it's individual. There is no one way to look beautiful, and anyone who tries to tell you otherwise is simply wrong.

Embracing body positivity means giving yourself permission to exist in the skin you're in without apology. It means showing up, living your life fully, wearing what you want, doing what you love, and not waiting for some magical day when you're "good enough" by someone else's standards. You're already good enough. You're already beautiful. And when you carry yourself with that truth in mind, others will see it too.

Setting Boundaries and Standing Firm

Now, if there's one thing I want you to take to heart, it's this: setting boundaries isn't selfish. It's necessary. Too often, we're taught to be polite, to keep the peace, to make sure everyone else is comfortable—even at the cost of our own well-being. But let me tell you, there is real power in learning to say "no." There is strength in protecting your energy, in valuing your time, in refusing to let others drain you.

Setting boundaries is about knowing your worth. When you say "no" to something that doesn't serve you, you're saying "yes" to yourself. And that is one of the most empowering things you can do. Boundaries are not walls; they're guidelines for how you deserve to be treated. They're your way of saying, "This is what I need to thrive. This is what I will and won't tolerate."

Learning to stand firm in those boundaries takes courage, especially if you're used to being a people-pleaser. It might feel uncomfortable at first. You might worry about disappointing others or being seen as difficult. But remember, those who truly care about you will respect your boundaries. And those who don't? They were never really in your corner to begin with. Boundaries are a way to separate the people who are genuinely supportive from those who are simply taking advantage.

So, start small. Practice saying "no" in situations where it feels safe, and build up from there. The more you do it, the more natural it will feel. And don't just set boundaries with others—set them with yourself. Recognize when you're overcommitting, when you're pushing yourself too hard, when you're not giving yourself the rest you need. Boundaries are about self-respect, and they start from within.

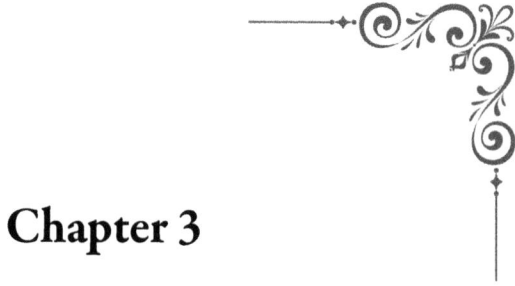

Chapter 3

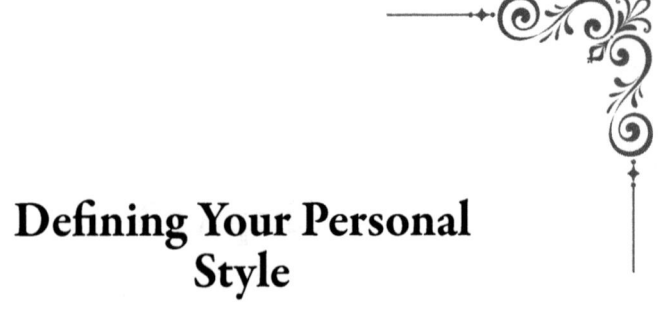

Defining Your Personal Style

Finding Your Fashion Personality

Let's talk about style—your personal style. And by "personal," I mean something that genuinely reflects who **you** are, not who someone else thinks you should be. Fashion is one of the most immediate ways we communicate who we are to the world. It's not about labels or fitting into a trend; it's about showing up in a way that feels true to you. So, first things first, we've got to tap into what makes you, **you.**

Finding your fashion personality is a journey of self-discovery, just like any other part of your identity. Maybe you're drawn to bold, statement-making pieces that speak before you even say a word. Or perhaps you lean towards a classic, timeless look—elegant and understated, but powerful in its simplicity. Maybe you're eclectic, mixing and matching styles and colors like it's an art form. Whatever it is, there's no right or wrong here. The goal is to identify what feels most authentic to you and lean into it unapologetically.

Start by asking yourself what you feel good in. Think about the times you've looked in the mirror and thought, **Yes, this is me.** What were you wearing? How did it make you feel? Comfort and confidence are two things that should always be part of your style equation. If it doesn't feel comfortable, if it doesn't make you feel like the best version of yourself, then it's not your style—it's just a costume. And we're not here to play dress-up; we're here to own our space.

AND LISTEN, DON'T BE afraid to experiment. Finding your style is an evolving process, just like anything else in life. You don't have to have it all figured out in one day, one month, or even one year. Try different things. See what resonates with you, and don't be afraid to step outside your comfort zone. Sometimes you've got to push the boundaries a bit to see where you really fit. The key is to pay attention to what feels right and what doesn't. Your style should feel like a natural extension of who you are, not something you're trying to force.

Fashion Fundamentals: Building a Wardrobe

Now, once you've got a sense of your fashion personality, it's time to build a wardrobe that reflects it. Here's the truth: you don't need a closet full of clothes to look good or feel good. You just need a few key pieces that you can mix and match to create a variety of looks. It's about quality, versatility, and making smart choices. Your wardrobe should be your toolkit, a collection that gives you the freedom to express yourself without overthinking it.

Start with the basics. Every wardrobe needs a few foundational pieces—things like a well-fitting pair of jeans, a blazer that makes you feel like a boss, a classic white shirt that you can dress up or down, and a comfortable pair of shoes that you can walk in for hours. These aren't just clothes; they're your staples, the pieces that ground your style. You build around them, layer them, mix them up, and make them your own. When you've got the fundamentals in place, you'll find it so much easier to put together outfits that feel like **you**.

And don't feel like you have to buy everything all at once. Building a wardrobe is a process. Be intentional with each piece you add. Ask yourself, "Does this fit with my style? Will I actually wear this, or am I just buying it because it's on sale or because everyone else is wearing it?" Remember, this is *your* wardrobe, your personal collection of pieces that tell your story. You don't need to impress anyone else with it. The only person you're dressing for is you.

When you shop, think in terms of versatility. Can that dress you're eyeing be worn to work, to dinner, and even on the weekend? Can that jacket be paired with a dress just as easily as with jeans? The more flexible your wardrobe, the easier it'll be to adapt to whatever life throws at you, and the less you'll feel like you have "nothing to wear." Think of your closet as a toolkit for self-expression. You're building a collection of items that let you show up as your most authentic self, no matter the occasion.

Accessorizing with Purpose

I know, they might seem like the little things, but don't underestimate the power of a good accessory. A statement necklace, a favorite pair of earrings, a bold bag—these are the things that can take an outfit from basic to unforgettable. But here's the thing: accessorizing is about enhancing, not overpowering. You want your accessories to complement your look, not define it.

When you're choosing accessories, think about what message you're trying to send. Are you going for a polished, sophisticated look? Opt for classic pieces that add a touch of elegance, like a simple pair of pearl earrings or a sleek watch. Want to show a bit of personality? Go for something bold and unique—maybe a chunky bracelet or a colorful scarf. Accessories are a chance to add a personal touch, to bring a little extra "you" into your outfit.

And remember, less is often more. You don't need to pile on everything at once. Sometimes, a single statement piece can have more impact than wearing every accessory you own. Trust your instincts. If it feels like too much, it probably is. Keep it simple, keep it intentional, and make sure every piece you wear has a purpose. You're not just throwing things on for the sake of it; you're building a look that says something about who you are.

And don't forget about practical accessories. A good bag is not just an accessory; it's a necessity. You want something that looks good, but that's also functional. Same goes for shoes. Sure, those heels might look fabulous, but if you can't walk in them, they're not worth it. The best accessories are the ones that work with you, not against you. Choose pieces that add to your confidence, not take away from it.

Chapter 4

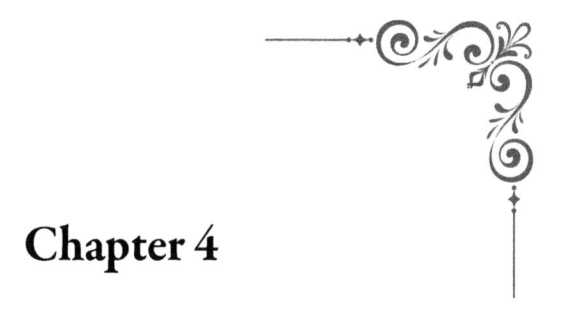

Celebrating Cultural Heritage in Style

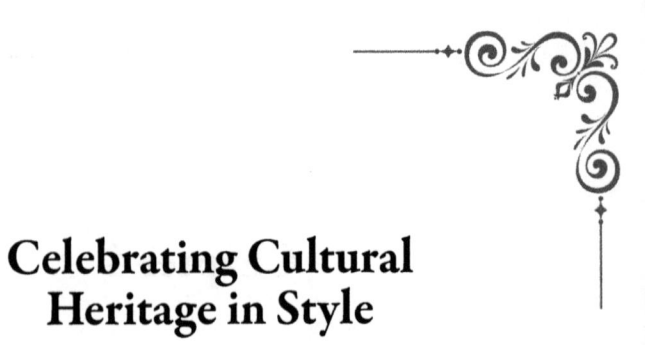

Incorporating Cultural Elements into Your Wardrobe

When you step into the world of fashion, you don't just wear clothing; you tell a story. Every piece has a narrative, a heritage, a heartbeat of its own. So, how do you blend traditional elements with contemporary fashion? It's all about balance, my friends.

Start with your foundation pieces. Think about those classic jeans or a chic white blouse that you love. Now, imagine layering them with a bright kente cloth scarf or a dashiki shirt. Those bold colors and intricate designs breathe life into basic outfits. You see, it's not just about pairing; it's about creating a dialogue between the past and the present.

Now, let's not forget about accessories! They're the unsung heroes of your wardrobe. A statement necklace made from traditional beads can transform a simple outfit into something that resonates. You can mix and match a sleek leather jacket with a flowing African print skirt. It's that effortless juxtaposition that speaks volumes about who you are.

And shoes? Oh, let's not skimp on the shoes. A pair of modern ankle boots can elevate a handwoven dress, merging traditional craftsmanship with contemporary chic. When you're out and about, that little bit of heritage peeking through your ensemble becomes a conversation starter. People notice. They want to know more, and that's your opportunity to share your roots and inspire others.

Don't be afraid to experiment. Fashion should be fun! If you have a family heirloom, like a beautiful brooch or a woven belt, integrate it into your daily wear. It's a celebration of your history, your family, and it's a chance to shine a light on your unique heritage.

Understanding the Stories Behind Fabrics

Each textile carries with it a history, a cultural significance that dates back generations. Take, for instance, the rich history of indigo dyeing in West Africa. This practice has not only produced stunning fabrics but also symbolizes deep cultural roots. It's about more than just aesthetics; it's about honoring the artistry of those who came before us.

Every pattern tells a story, every color has meaning. The intricate designs of African wax prints reflect the diversity and vibrancy of the cultures they represent. The motifs can convey messages about identity, community, and resilience. When you wear a fabric with such significance, you're not just making a fashion statement; you're embodying a legacy.

Let's also look at the significance of textiles like silk, which has been revered in various cultures, from Asia to Europe. The stories of silk production are filled with traditions and craftsmanship that have been passed down through generations. Understanding these stories enriches your appreciation for what you wear. When you slip into a silk dress, it's not just luxurious; it's a testament to the skill and dedication of artisans who have crafted these materials through centuries.

You should also consider where your fabrics come from. Support brands that honor traditional practices and promote ethical sourcing. When you do, you contribute to the preservation of these cultural narratives. You're not just a consumer; you're a steward of culture, participating in a movement that values sustainability and respect for artisans.

Making a Statement with Tradition

When you wear culturally inspired pieces, you're not just showing off beautiful fabrics and designs; you're making a bold declaration of who you are. You embrace your roots and showcase them with pride. That's powerful, my friends.

Take the plunge and wear that stunning kimono or that gorgeous sari. Don't wait for a special occasion. Every day is an opportunity to honor your culture. Pair a traditional garment with modern silhouettes. That's where the magic happens. Imagine walking into a room wearing a beautifully tailored blazer over a flowing African print dress. You're not just turning heads; you're sparking conversations.

Remember, the goal is to wear these pieces confidently. When you step out in garments that reflect your heritage, wear them like a crown. Stand tall. Own your story. Your cultural identity is your superpower.

Let's also not forget the art of layering. A simple white tee can become a canvas for cultural expression when you add a colorful wrap or an embroidered vest. It's all about creating layers of meaning. Your outfit becomes a conversation piece, a reflection of your journey and the influences that shape you.

And when you do wear traditional pieces, consider how you can elevate them. Add modern accessories that reflect your personal style. A sleek pair of hoops or a bold clutch can provide that touch of contemporary flair while still honoring your roots. You become a bridge between the old and the new, celebrating tradition while embracing innovation.

You have the power to redefine cultural fashion. Let's challenge the stereotypes. When you dress unapologetically, you inspire others to do the same. You encourage conversations about identity, diversity, and acceptance. Your style can spark a movement, showing that it's possible to be rooted in your culture while navigating the modern world with grace and elegance.

So, step into your closet with intention. Choose pieces that resonate with your spirit and honor your heritage. Celebrate the stories behind your clothing and wear them with pride. Let your wardrobe be a testament to the richness of your culture, the beauty of your identity, and the strength of your voice.

Chapter 5

Navigating Trends and Staying True to Yourself

Trends vs. Timeless: Choosing What's Right for You

We all know that the fashion world moves at lightning speed, with new trends popping up almost daily. It's easy to get swept away in the latest frenzy, feeling like you need to keep up or risk falling behind. But here's the truth: you don't have to sacrifice who you are for a fleeting trend. The key lies in balance.

Start by identifying what defines your core style. What pieces make you feel like the best version of yourself? It might be that tailored blazer that gives you confidence or those vintage jeans that make you feel effortlessly chic. Once you've identified those staples, use them as your anchor. When a new trend emerges, ask yourself: Does this resonate with me? Can I see this working with my current wardrobe? If the answer is yes, then welcome it in. If not, let it pass.

This doesn't mean you can't experiment with trends. In fact, I encourage it! Incorporate trendy pieces in small doses. A vibrant statement top or a unique accessory can add freshness to your wardrobe without overshadowing your essence. You don't want to become a walking billboard for every trend. Instead, you want to enhance your style with elements that speak to you.

Remember, true style is about expressing who you are, not just mirroring what's on the runway. If a trend feels forced or doesn't align with your spirit, it's okay to sit it out. When you wear something that doesn't resonate with you, it shows. Confidence stems from authenticity. So, stay true to yourself, and the world will see that shine through.

Social Media Pressure and Authenticity

Social media can be a double-edged sword. On one hand, it's a platform for inspiration and connection; on the other, it can be a breeding ground for comparison and self-doubt. As you scroll through feeds filled with perfectly curated outfits, it's easy to fall into the trap of comparing yourself to those influencers or peers who seem to have it all together. But here's the real talk: what you see online is often a highlight reel, not the full story.

First and foremost, recognize that you are not alone in feeling this pressure. We all experience it to some degree, and it's completely natural. The key is to approach social media with intention. Use it as a tool for inspiration rather than a measuring stick for your worth. Follow accounts that uplift you, celebrate diversity, and resonate with your values. Curate your feed to reflect positivity and authenticity.

Next, practice gratitude for your unique journey. Take a moment to reflect on what makes your style yours. Celebrate those quirks and idiosyncrasies that set you apart from others. Your journey is a mosaic of experiences that no one else can replicate. Focus on that rather than the seemingly flawless lives of others.

Also, remember that it's okay to take breaks from social media when it feels overwhelming. Step back and reconnect with yourself. Engage in activities that bring you joy and allow your creative spirit to flourish without the influence of others. Paint, write, dance—whatever feeds your soul. By nurturing your individuality, you strengthen your authenticity, which is far more powerful than any trendy outfit.

Finally, when you do post, do so from a place of genuineness. Share your unique perspective, your journey, and your style without the pressure to conform. Embrace the messiness of life and the beautiful imperfections that come with it. When you showcase your true self, you encourage others to do the same, creating a ripple effect of authenticity.

Curating Your Own Style Inspiration Board

Let's create something truly special—a style inspiration board that reflects who you are. This isn't just about gathering pretty pictures; it's about crafting a visual narrative that captures your essence. Whether you go digital or physical, this board should be a sanctuary for your style ideas, dreams, and inspirations.

Start by collecting images that resonate with you. These can be fashion photos, colors, textures, or even quotes that inspire you. Look for pieces that ignite a spark in your heart and make you feel alive. What do you gravitate toward? What makes you smile? Use those feelings as your guide.

Next, consider the stories behind the visuals. Why does a particular outfit resonate with you? Is it the vibrant colors, the cut, or perhaps the confidence it exudes? Dig deep into your motivations. This process is about more than just aesthetics; it's about understanding yourself on a deeper level. What you choose to include in your inspiration board should reflect not just the latest trends but your personal journey, aspirations, and values.

Once you have your collection, arrange the images in a way that feels harmonious. This is your space, so let your creativity flow. If you're working digitally, there are plenty of platforms that allow you to easily drag and drop images. If you prefer a physical board, grab a poster or corkboard and start pinning away. Don't worry about perfection—embrace the beauty of spontaneity!

As you curate your board, allow it to evolve over time. Update it regularly with new inspirations and remove what no longer resonates. This is a living reflection of you, and like you, it should grow and change.

Finally, use your inspiration board as a compass for your wardrobe choices. When you're unsure about an outfit, turn to your board. Let it remind you of your style roots and inspire you to experiment with new combinations that feel true to you. You're not just curating a collection of images; you're crafting a blueprint for your personal style journey.

Fashion is a powerful tool for self-expression, and by navigating trends while staying true to yourself, you create a narrative that's uniquely yours. Celebrate your journey, embrace your heritage, and let your style be a testament to your authenticity.

Chapter 6

Becoming the Best Version of Yourself

Daily Habits for Confidence and Self-Care

Embracing your journey toward becoming the best version of yourself starts with the small, everyday choices you make. Confidence doesn't just appear; it's cultivated through consistent self-care practices. Let's explore the daily habits that empower you and help you stay grounded.

Begin your day with intention. When you wake up, take a moment to breathe deeply and set a positive affirmation for yourself. It could be as simple as, "I am worthy," or "I embrace my unique journey." Speak it aloud. There's power in your words, and starting your day with this mindset sets a tone of self-love and acceptance.

Incorporate movement into your morning routine, whether it's a brisk walk, yoga, or even a dance party in your living room. Find joy in movement. It doesn't have to be a rigorous workout; what matters is that it makes you feel alive. This practice not only gets your blood flowing but also boosts your mood and confidence.

Next, prioritize nourishing your body with wholesome foods. A balanced breakfast can fuel you for the day ahead. Think about how certain foods make you feel—choose those that energize and inspire you. Remember, you're not just feeding your body; you're fueling your spirit.

As the day progresses, carve out time for self-reflection. Journaling can be a powerful tool for growth. Write down your thoughts, aspirations, and even your struggles. This practice helps you process your feelings and track your journey. Celebrate your wins, no matter how small, and acknowledge the challenges you overcome. This reflection fosters resilience and self-awareness.

Make self-care a non-negotiable part of your routine. Whether it's enjoying a long bath, meditating, or indulging in a favorite hobby, find moments to nurture your soul. These practices are essential for recharging your spirit and fostering a strong sense of self. When you take care of yourself, you radiate confidence that others can feel.

Finally, surround yourself with positive energy. The people you interact with greatly influence your mindset. Seek out those who uplift and inspire you, and distance yourself from negativity. Building a supportive community creates a powerful environment that nurtures your growth and confidence.

Setting Goals and Staying Motivated

Goals give you direction; they're your roadmap to becoming your best self. But how do you set goals that resonate with you and keep the fire of motivation burning?

Start by visualizing what you want to achieve. Think about both personal and style-related aspirations. Maybe you want to develop a signature look or embark on a journey toward personal growth. Be specific about what these goals look like. The clearer your vision, the more empowered you will feel to pursue it.

Break your goals down into manageable steps. If you want to revamp your wardrobe, start by decluttering. Identify what you love and what no longer serves you. From there, create a shopping list of versatile pieces that align with your vision. Small, actionable steps build momentum, making it easier to stay motivated.

Set deadlines for your goals to create a sense of urgency. Deadlines encourage you to prioritize your aspirations and keep you accountable. However, be flexible with yourself. Life happens, and it's essential to adapt and recalibrate when necessary. Progress is not always linear, and that's perfectly okay.

To keep your motivation alive, track your progress. Celebrate milestones along the way. Every time you achieve a goal, big or small, acknowledge it. Reward yourself with something meaningful—maybe a day off or a special treat. These celebrations reinforce your commitment to your journey.

Surround yourself with reminders of your goals. Create a vision board that visually represents your aspirations. Pin up images that inspire you, quotes that resonate, and symbols of the style you want to cultivate. Your board becomes a constant source of motivation, encouraging you to keep pushing forward.

Lastly, don't hesitate to share your goals with others. When you voice your aspirations, you invite support and accountability into your journey. Find an accountability partner or join a community that shares your interests. These connections can provide motivation and encouragement when you need it most.

Giving Back and Inspiring Others

As you work toward becoming the best version of yourself, remember that your journey is not just about you. It's about lifting others as you rise. Embracing your growth journey means sharing your confidence with those around you and inspiring others to embark on their paths.

Start by identifying ways to give back to your community. This could be mentoring someone, sharing your knowledge through workshops, or simply being a supportive friend. Your experiences hold immense value, and when you share them, you empower others to see their potential.

Consider the power of storytelling. Your journey, with all its ups and downs, can serve as inspiration for others. When you open up about your struggles and triumphs, you create a space for vulnerability and authenticity. People relate to stories—they see themselves in your experiences and realize they're not alone.

Lead by example. Show others how you embrace your cultural heritage, practice self-care, and stay true to your values. When you embody confidence and authenticity, you naturally inspire those around you. Your actions speak louder than words, and they can ignite a spark in someone else's journey.

As you grow, also remember to advocate for diversity and inclusion. Support brands and initiatives that uplift marginalized voices in the fashion industry. By amplifying diverse perspectives, you contribute to a more inclusive narrative that celebrates all identities.

Finally, encourage others to share their stories. Create spaces where individuals feel safe to express themselves, whether in person or online. When we share our journeys, we build connections that foster community and support.

By giving back and inspiring others, you not only enrich your life but also contribute to the growth of those around you. Together, we can create a world where everyone feels empowered to embrace their uniqueness and strive for their best selves.

Conclusion

Life is this intricate tapestry, woven with threads of dreams, struggles, and triumphs. Each moment shapes who we are, guiding us along our unique paths. It's vital to embrace every color, every twist, and turn of our stories. As we navigate this world, remember: authenticity is your greatest asset. Be unapologetic about your journey; let it shine through your choices and the way you carry yourself. Own your narrative because no one else can tell it like you can.

You've got a wealth of experiences that no one else can replicate. Each challenge you've faced, every victory, and even the moments of uncertainty—they all add depth to your character. Recognize the power in your voice, in your story. There's strength in vulnerability; when you share your truth, you create connections. You inspire others to stand tall in their own stories, to find courage in their struggles.

Fashion isn't merely about clothing; it's a powerful form of expression. It's about declaring who you are, where you come from, and what you stand for. Incorporating cultural elements into your wardrobe isn't just a trend; it's a celebration of identity. It's about honoring those who came before you while paving the way for those who will follow. Let your clothes tell a story—your story. The patterns, the colors, the textures—they all have histories worth sharing. Each time you step out, wear your culture with pride and let the world see the beauty of your heritage.

Navigating trends can feel overwhelming, but remember: it's not about losing yourself in the latest fashions. It's about blending what's trendy with your core values and style. Take what resonates with you and leave behind what doesn't. Social media can amplify voices but also create noise. Focus on what speaks to your heart, not just what fills your feed. Authenticity shines brightest when it's rooted in your own identity. Curate your style inspiration from what inspires you, not what others dictate.

Set goals that align with your passions. Your ambitions are a reflection of your journey and your unique vision for the future. Stay motivated, even when the path gets rocky. Surround yourself with people who uplift you, who challenge you to reach higher. Celebrate every milestone; no achievement is too small to acknowledge. By doing so, you reinforce your commitment to growth.

The most profound impact often comes from lifting others as you rise. As you grow, look for ways to give back. Share your knowledge, your successes, and even your failures. When you inspire others to embrace their potential, you create a ripple effect of empowerment. Imagine a community where everyone feels seen, heard, and valued—what a beautiful world that would be! Advocate for diversity, inclusion, and representation in every space you inhabit. Your voice is a tool for change, so use it to uplift those around you.

You have the ability to make a difference—not just for yourself but for others too. Encourage those around you to express their individuality and share their stories. Create spaces where everyone feels welcome to explore their identities. This is where true growth happens, where we learn from each other and cultivate understanding and compassion.

Life isn't about perfection; it's about progress. Embrace the messiness of it all—the stumbles, the missteps, and the unexpected twists. Every experience contributes to your growth. Take risks, step outside your comfort zone, and be open to learning. The journey is filled with lessons that shape your character and fortify your resilience.

AS YOU MOVE FORWARD, remember that your journey doesn't end here. It's a continuous process of discovery and growth. Keep pushing boundaries, challenging the status quo, and rewriting the narrative. You have the power to create a legacy that inspires generations to come. Be bold, be brave, and be unapologetically you. Stand firm in your truth and walk through the world with grace and confidence.

In every aspect of your life, infuse passion and purpose. Seek out what ignites your spirit and dive into it wholeheartedly. Surround yourself with things and people that reflect your values, that inspire you to be better, to strive for more. It's not just about personal success; it's about uplifting others along the way.

In closing, remember that your story is still being written. You are the author of your life. Embrace the pen, and don't shy away from the tough chapters or the unexpected plot twists. They all play a role in shaping who you are. Let your legacy be one of authenticity, empowerment, and unwavering strength. When you look back on your life, may you feel pride in the journey you've taken and the impact you've made.

Go forth and shine your light brightly. The world needs your voice, your story, and your unique perspective. Be the change you wish to see, and inspire others to do the same. Embrace your heritage, cultivate your passions, and share your gifts with the world. You have the power to make waves, to inspire change, and to celebrate every beautiful facet of who you are. So, step boldly into your future, knowing that you are not just a part of this world—you are a force to be reckoned with.

Unagologetically You!

Don't miss out!

Visit the website below and you can sign up to receive emails whenever LILIAN M. publishes a new book. There's no charge and no obligation.

https://books2read.com/r/B-A-VWNSC-NXKGF

BOOKS 2 READ

Connecting independent readers to independent writers.